C000146857

To

_____

From

_____

Date

_____

It was nice growing up
with someone like you—
someone to lean on,
someone to count on . . .
someone to tell on!
—Author Unknown

A Gift Book for Sisters and Those Who Wish to Celebrate Them

What If There Were No Sisters?

Caron Chandler Loveless
Illustrations by Dennis Hill

HOWARD BOOKS
A DIVISION OF SIMON & SCHUSTER
New York   London   Toronto   Sydney

If suddenly there were no sisters, for real.

Gone! Just like that! Wonder how it would feel?

For a time, right at first, it might seem really neat,
Get the folks to myself; that could be pretty sweet.

No sharing Mom while shopping 'til dark
And Dad to myself for long walks in the park.

If there were no sisters, think what this could mean:
Both sides of my room might finally stay clean!

When company came I could have the whole bed,
Not fight for the right to one half of the spread.

But before very long this could fail to be fun.
If sisters go AWOL I'd sure miss a ton.

Who'd share in my birthdays as I celebrate?
Help me open my gifts and pile cake on my plate?
On long rainy days when there's nothing to do
Who would think of charades, Go Fish, or of Clue?

And who'd be around when my friends went away?

Who would say, "That's okay, 'cause I'm here to stay."

With no sister to help, who'd plan our great plays,

And with fun music blasting, who'd sing right along

Sharing microphone hairbrushes song after song?

Who would be with me to laugh 'til we cried
Recalling that time when my hairdo got fried?

Whole pages in albums I'd have to delete.

With no matching outfits they'd seem incomplete.

Our whole family story would come up quite short.
Without sisters talking there's less to report.

And where would I go with deep secrets to tell?

No sisters to hear when things didn't go well.

Who would say the right
thing without taking a pause,

And who, with great love,
would tell me the truth
As we struggle together
to get through our youth?

Who would be at my wedding, smiling through tears?
Who'd fix my mascara? Who'd calm all my fears?

If there were no sisters, a crisis would mount.
The loss to my life would be too high to count.

While there have been moments

I wanted to scream,

Hear me shout now:

We make a great team!

With you my life's richer,

let there be no doubt

You, my sweet sister,

I Can't Live Without!

"I thank my God every time I remember you."
—Philippians 1:3

Sister, I couldn't live without you because:

_____

_____

_____

_____

_____

_____

_____

_____

_____

_____

_____

Our purpose at Howard Books is to:
• *Increase faith* in the hearts of growing Christians
• *Inspire holiness* in the lives of believers
• *Instill hope* in the hearts of struggling people everywhere
Because He's coming again!

Published by Howard Books, a division of Simon & Schuster, Inc.
1230 Avenue of the Americas, New York, NY 10020
www.howardpublishing.com

What If There Were No Sisters? © 2009 by Caron Chandler Loveless

ISBN-13: 978-1-4165-5198-0
ISBN-10:   1-4165-5198-0

10 9 8 7 6 5 4 3 2 1

Manufactured in China

For information regarding special discounts for bulk purchases, please contact: Simon & Schuster Special Sales at 1-866-506-1949 or business@simonandschuster.com.

The Simon & Schuster Speakers Bureau can bring authors to your live event. For more information or to book an event contact the Simon & Schuster Speakers Bureau at 1-866-248-3049 or visit our website at www.simonspeakers.com.

Edited by Chrys Howard
Cover design by Stephanie D. Walker
Interior design by Dennis Hill and Stephanie D. Walker
Illustrations by Dennis Hill

Sister, I couldn't live without you because:

_____

_____

_____

_____

_____

_____

_____

_____

_____

Our purpose at Howard Books is to:
• *Increase faith* in the hearts of growing Christians
• *Inspire holiness* in the lives of believers
• *Instill hope* in the hearts of struggling people everywhere
Because He's coming again!

Published by Howard Books, a division of Simon & Schuster, Inc.
1230 Avenue of the Americas, New York, NY 10020
www.howardpublishing.com

What If There Were No Sisters? © 2009 by Caron Chandler Loveless

ISBN-13: 978-1-4165-5198-0
ISBN-10:   1-4165-5198-0

10 9 8 7 6 5 4 3 2 1

Manufactured in China

For information regarding special discounts for bulk purchases, please contact: Simon & Schuster Special Sales at 1-866-506-1949 or business@simonandschuster.com.

The Simon & Schuster Speakers Bureau can bring authors to your live event. For more information or to book an event contact the Simon & Schuster Speakers Bureau at 1-866-248-3049 or visit our website at www.simonspeakers.com.

Edited by Chrys Howard
Cover design by Stephanie D. Walker
Interior design by Dennis Hill and Stephanie D. Walker
Illustrations by Dennis Hill